The SACRED

LANGUAGE of

COLOUR

It is the quality of a ray life – manifesting in time and space – which determines the phenomenal appearance.

Bailey 1951, 26

The SACRED LANGUAGE of COLOUR

A GUIDE FOR LIVING IN

the WORLD of MEANING

D A Sheridan

D A SHERIDAN

2021

Copyright © 2021 D A Sheridan. All rights reserved.
This book, or any portion thereof, may not be reproduced or used in any way whatsoever without the written permission of the publisher except for brief quotations in a book review or scholarly journal. For further information, contact the publisher at dasheri@outlook.com.
First published 2018. Second edition 2021.
ISBN 978-0-6482683-2-1

IMAGES
Abstract Stones And Water, 19 © Can Stock Photo/Elenaray.
Aura-Soma Equilibrium, 3 © D A Sheridan.
Bird Nest, 54 © Can Stock Photo/Elenaray.
Chakra Energy Field, cover © Can Stock Photo/Elenaray.
Colour Wheel Vector, 21 © Can Stock Photo/PeterHermesFurian.
Concealed Empath, 28 © Can Stock Photo/Elenaray.
Dividers Design, 2, 17, 52 © Can Stock Photo/oliska.
Fifth Ray of Concrete Knowledge, 39 © D A Sheridan.
First Ray of Will or Power, 35 © D A Sheridan.
Fourth Ray of Harmony Through Conflict, 38 © D A Sheridan.
Generosity, 14 © Can Stock Photo/Elenaray.
Joy And Faith, 6 © Can Stock Photo/Elenaray.
Second Ray of Love Wisdom, 36 © D A Sheridan.
Seventh Ray of Ceremonial Order, 41 © D A Sheridan.
Sixth Ray of Idealism or Devotion, 40 © D A Sheridan.
Soul Cleansing, 62 © Can Stock Photo/Elenaray.
Third Ray of Abstract Intelligence & Activity, 37 © D A Sheridan.
Vector Abstract Background With Waves, 3 © Can Stock Photo
    /NatalyaLevish (adapted).
Vector Page & Book Decor And Design Elements, 1, 7, 13, 20, 29, 42,
    55 © Can Stock Photo/Sergo.
Visionary Ruin, 46 © Can Stock Photo/Elenaray.
White Horse, 51 © Can Stock Photo/Elenaray.
Yellow Butterfly, 59 © Can Stock Photo/Elenaray.
Yoga Lotus Pose Padmasana With Colored Chakra Points, 11 © Can
    Stock Photo/JackyBrown.
Zodiac Astrology Vector, 24, 43 © Can Stock Photo/PeterHermes
    Furian (adapted).

Table of Contents

INTRODUCTION	1
PROTECTION, DEDICATION & MEDITATION	7
THE SOUL	13
A CIRCLE IS A CIRCLE	20
ESOTERIC ASTROLOGY	29
COLOUR & ASTROLOGY	42
COLOUR KEY WORDS	55
BIBLIOGRAPHY	66

Table of Figures

Colour Wheel	21
Zodiac Wheel	24
Exoteric Words for Zodiac Signs	26
The Seven Rays	33
Planets & Rays	34
First Ray of Will or Power	35
Second Ray of Love Wisdom	36
Third Ray of Abstract Intelligence & Activity	37
Fourth Ray of Harmony Through Conflict	38
Fifth Ray of Concrete Knowledge	39
Sixth Ray of Idealism or Devotion	40
Seventh Ray of Ceremonial Order	41
Zodiac Colour Wheel	43
Esoteric Words for Zodiac Signs	44

Dedicated with gratitude to my teachers, especially those on the other side who prompted and helped to complete this text, to my dear companions with whom I walk the path and those beautiful, shining, creative souls who are my children for their immeasurable love and support.

Thou canst not travel on the Path

before thou hast become that Path itself.

H.P.B. 1889, 12

Introduction

Mine was an idyllic childhood growing up on a small, remote island in the South Pacific Ocean. Mum was always (and still is) our rock – a kind-hearted, generous woman who ensured my siblings and I regularly attended Sunday school and youth fellowship – while dad could be described as the problematic father. At 13, I was sent to a Church of England boarding school in rural Australia which actually put me off religion, but probably provided the conditions during those formative years that enabled me to develop into the strong, independent person I am today. At 15, I left school, completed a secretarial course (the shortest I could find) and, by the age of 22, I'd visited Europe three times.

At 23, I received knowledge from Maharaji (now known as Prem Rawat), began to meditate and, for the next few years, participated joyfully in satsang and service in various countries while I travelled. In 1984 in Sydney the first of my four children arrived, a beautiful baby girl. For five years, as a stay-at-home mum, I provided high quality care for my growing family – my daughter and two high spirited sons born in the late 1980s. In 1997 the often fraught relationship of 16 years between the children's father and I collapsed, and soon after that I discovered Alice Bailey's texts. Many days were spent wholly engaged poring through Esoteric Psychology I and II and other works. Before long I'd enrolled as a student of The Arcane School, a non-sectarian school for esoteric studies established by Alice Bailey, where I commenced occult meditation (Raja yoga) and eventually mentored other students whilst involved in the activities of Sydney Goodwill.

I first saw Aura-Soma Equilibrium at a Mind Body Spirit festival in 1999. Immediately drawn to these vibrant, dual coloured bottles, the "jewels" of the Aura-Soma colour care system, I quickly completed practitioner training levels 1, 2 and 3 the following year. Fuelled by aspiration, I sold my Toyota Celica – my most cherished possession – and opened a small natural therapies practice in Sydney's south; however, a personal crisis soon developed forcing its premature closure.

Next, time was spent consolidating and reassessing what was important in life. Wanting to align my inner spiritual life with my outer worldly activities and yearning to be able to make a difference, at the age of 45 I enrolled at university and acquired qualifications in teaching and counselling. In 2008 my daughter, aged 6, accompanied me to the Northern Territory where I taught indigenous students at a remote school for two years. Upon returning to Sydney I continued to teach, mainly gifted and talented students; then moved into community work where I worked with children in foster care and as a voluntary telephone counsellor for several years.

Examination of the literature concerning Alice Bailey (1880-1949) reveals her affiliation with the Theosophical Society, her absolute conviction of the interconnectedness of all things and her deep concern for human betterment. In her seminal thesis *The Texts of Alice A Bailey: An Inquiry into the Role of Esotericism in Transforming Consciousness,* Isobel Wightman (2006, 1) describes Alice

Bailey as a twentieth century esoteric thinker who acted merely as the scribe of Tibetan master Djwhal Khul, a spiritual master of the Ageless Wisdom. In November 1919 Djwhal Khul made contact with Alice Bailey asking her to write for him in order to publish certain books. Disliking the so-called occult literature distributed at that time, Alice Bailey initially refused then agreed to a trial of one month when Djwhal Khul explained that telepathic rapport was a proven phenomenon and a matter of scientific interest. Between 1919 and 1949 Alice Bailey wrote 24 volumes on esoteric philosophy, 19 of which were written in collaboration with Djwhal Khul, and established several organizations – The Arcane School, World Goodwill and Triangles – that operate to this day on a global scale. Lucis Publishing Company continues to print her texts.

In her *Unfinished Autobiography*, Alice Bailey (1951, 53-57) recounts how from her conservative British background and as an evangelical Christian she worked in soldiers' homes for the British army in Ireland and British-ruled India in the early 1900s. After a breakdown, she moved to California where three children were born into a troubled marriage. When her husband eventually left, impoverished Bailey worked in a sardine factory to support her family. During this difficult time, she met two English women from the Theosophical Society. Inspired by the Society's teachings, Alice Bailey adopted the esoteric worldview presented by the tradition.

Alice Bailey's cosmology is an extended reformulation of Helena Blavatsky's *The Secret Doctrine*. Her teaching regarding the subtle constitution of man is based on the notion that an individual is made up of a personality (comprised of physical, emotional and mental bodies), soul and monad (or spiritual triad). Alice Bailey proffers the view that evolution leads to synthesis, integration and intelligent cooperation of the individual for the good of the whole and, to achieve this, the personality undergoes a reorientation whereby control of the personality is relinquished to the soul. The path is then traced back from whence it came.

The Great Invocation, shared by Djwhal Khul and Alice Bailey in the books they co-produced, was given to all humanity by the Spiritual Hierarchy in April 1945. Voicing the destiny and divine plan for humanity in the coming age, the beauty and strength of *The Great Invocation* (Lucis n.d.) lie in its simplicity and expression of certain central truths. A means of alignment, it is said that working with this powerful invocation creates great shifts in character, attitudes, goals and intentions.

The Great Invocation

From the point of Light within the Mind of God
Let light stream forth into human minds.
Let Light descend on Earth.

From the point of Love within the Heart of God
Let love stream forth into human hearts.
May the Coming One return to Earth.

From the centre where the Will of God is known
Let purpose guide all little human wills –
The purpose which the Masters know and serve.

From the centre which we call the human race
Let the Plan of Love and Light work out
And may it seal the door where evil dwells.

Let Light and Love and Power restore the Plan on Earth.

Protection, Dedication & Meditation

Imagine a realm where the colours and hues of one's aura depict the substance of one's character, and where the underlying motives of all people are unfurled, like banners, for those who have eyes to see.
Instructions on Group Discipleship 2015, 19

The Aura-Soma colour care system is recognized by many as a soul therapy. There are five products that form the five pillars of this holistic, consciousness expanding system – the Equilibrium Oils, Pomanders, Quintessences, ArchAngeloi and Colour Essences.

Aura-Soma's founder, Vicky Wall (1918-1991) was physically blind; however, she was able to see auras and recognized that when people selected Aura-Soma Equilibrium they were drawn to bottles containing colours depleted from their own aura, the very colours needed to increase their sense of well-being. For this reason, her adage, "You are the colours you choose and these reflect your being's needs," is frequently quoted. Aura-Soma is for those who wish to remember the true essence of their inner or higher self.

Let's start in typical Aura-Soma fashion with *Protection, Dedication & Meditation*, a ritual begun by Vicky Wall who always commenced group sessions by sharing a Pomander amongst participants. Containing the energies of colour and 49 plants, Pomanders offer protection from negativity in your immediate environment and bring in the helpful, supportive qualities of their particular colour. After sharing the Pomander, Vicky (who created the first Original White Pomander in 1986) would light a candle, express a dedication and facilitate amazing meditations.

Try to integrate this ritual into your daily routine as, in addition to the benefits just mentioned, using a Pomander is an opportunity to send as an act of service the healing energy of colour to all humanity; whilst, from the viewpoint of your soul, it's an opportunity to ensure your seven main chakras, the energy centres of the "vehicle" it serves through, are aligned. To ensure you receive the most benefit possible, apply your Pomander lovingly and mindfully through your electro-magnetic field. To practice self-love in this way will help you feel nurtured and balanced, while you protect yourself from any surrounding negative energy and bring in the positive messages of the Pomander's colour. For example, applying the Red Pomander will help to boost your energy levels and feelings of being safely and securely grounded.

You may find, as I often do, while you perform this ritual intuitive insights can suddenly pop into consciousness as a result of the quiescent mind freeing space allowing them to appear. Performed regularly, this Pomander ritual will help you to develop mindfulness which, in turn, will help you experience more presence, or awareness of Spirit, in your life. Please note, this is an adapted method of applying an Aura-Soma Pomander – evolved as I've used this exquisite, holistic product on a daily basis for many years.

Pomander Ritual

Choose a Pomander you'd like to work with (select by colour or scent). Place three drops onto the palm of your left hand and rub your hands gently together. Stand straight, close your eyes, focus inwardly and raise your hands up above your head. Connect with Spirit and visualize a shower of white light, purifying and cleansing, passing through you – then offer the Pomander to the world: out of your left hand, around the entire planet irradiating the consciousness of all beings, and back into your right hand.

Now, with palms facing downward, hold both hands above your head. As it's the soul that expresses itself through colour, identify with your soul and offer the Pomander to the awaiting lower personality. Visualize the Pomander's essence falling gently into your crown chakra. Place your hands at the back of your head, the psychic gate, and offer the Pomander to all beings you've been in the past and will be in the future. Lovingly "oil the temple doors" by applying the Pomander with soft, circular strokes to your left and right temple areas intuitively sensing your aura while you do this.

Place the palms of your hands together as high as you can above your head then lower them mindfully down to your crown chakra. Visualize healing, spiritual energy emanating from its wide open violet petals. Hold the connection steady in the light.

Palms still together, lower both hands mindfully down to your third eye chakra. Visualize deep, mystical peace emanating from its wide open royal blue petals. Hold the connection steady in the light.

Lower both hands to your throat chakra. Visualize trust and peaceful communication emanating from its wide open blue petals. Hold the connection steady in the light.

Rest both hands gently over your heart chakra and offer the Pomander to any person or matter that weighs heavily on your heart. Visualize harmony and tranquility emanating from its wide open green petals. Be conscious of the inimitable beauty at the core of your being as you hold the connection steady in the light.

Lowering your hands mindfully again, place them lightly over your solar plexus chakra. Visualize the Pomander activating its bright yellow petals which open fully emitting shiny sparkles of happiness and confidence. Hold the connection steady in the light.

Place both hands lightly over your sacral chakra. Visualize bliss and deep joy emanating from its wide open orange petals. Hold the connection steady in the light.

Place both hands over your root chakra. Visualize yourself safely and securely grounded as passion, enthusiasm and vibrant energy emanate from its wide open red petals. Hold the connection steady in the light.

Palms facing downward, offer the Pomander to Earth. Ask Gaia to accept it. Visualize a thread of light linking your root chakra and Earth star, a minute point of light immediately beneath you within the Earth's surface. Hold the connection steady in the light.

Conclude the ritual with gentle, fluffing up gestures raising the Pomander's essence to shoulder height as you stand up straight. Affirm your intention to be mindful and present as you perform your daily tasks. Cup both hands over your face and inhale the Pomander, gratefully and deeply, three times.

Light a candle and articulate a dedication, anything close to your heart. For example, "I thank Vicky Wall for her incredible insight and gift that is Aura-Soma and dedicate today to healing and peace wherever it's needed through bringing more colour and light into the world." The simple ritual of lighting a candle is a profound act that enables you to invite Spirit and light into your life. The element of fire is a symbol of Spirit. Astrologically, the three fire signs – Aries, Leo and Sagittarius – form a triangle of intense spiritual energy within the zodiac wheel.

Finally, perform your meditation. There are many types of meditation so opt for one you're comfortable with.

An excellent method is to focus your attention at the highest point of your mental body and inwardly recite a positive affirmation as a seed thought. There's a window of opportunity, from two days before the full moon until two days after it, when those who are sensitive may be receptive to spiritual impression from higher realms. This is an opportune time to use an expression from Alice Bailey's esoteric Words for the Signs of the Zodiac as your seed thought (see page 44). When you meditate choose the statement for the zodiac sign the sun is currently passing through.

During meditation I intone *The Great Invocation* or similar mantrum such as the *Morning, Noon & Night Reflection* (Lucis n.d.) below. A potent tool to use with the current inflowing energies of the new age, when sounded correctly, a mantrum creates a funnel or vacuum in form which, in effect, is a direct line of communication between the one who sounds the mantrum and the one who is reached by its sound (Bailey 1922, 164).

Morning, Noon & Night Reflection

I stand a point of peace, and through the point which I can thus provide, love and true light can flow.

I stand in restful poise, and through that poise I can attract the gifts which I must give – an understanding heart, a quiet mind, myself.

I never am alone, for round me gather those I seek to serve, my brothers (and sisters) in the Ashram, souls that demand my help, e'en though I see them not, and those in distant places who seek the Master of my life, my brother, the Tibetan.

The Soul

Just as the hummingbird absorbs nectar from a flower, the sensitive soul absorbs light from beauty and its parallel manifestations: truth, which is beauty to the higher mind and goodness, which is beauty to the feeling nature.
Messages from Kanchenjunga 2015, 31

As the soul meditates deeply on its own plane, we recognize its reflection here on the physical plane as sacred shape, colour and sound. Symbolizing oneness, unlike the personality which acquires knowledge externally, the soul gains knowledge – and becomes wise – intuitively. The challenge, to achieve this inner knowing experience, is to develop sensitivity to soul impression to such a degree that you may register subtle intuitive insights consciously in your lower concrete mind. Once this feat is accomplished, you then face the conundrum of learning how to live as a soul in the world of the soul, or the "world of meaning" as it's referred to in the Ageless Wisdom.

All who tread the evolutionary path that eventually leads to enlightenment inevitably enter the world of meaning which, according to esoteric astrologer and teacher William Meader, "reveals the pattern of truth underlying outer circumstance." The world of meaning is a realm of consciousness used by the soul to convey its purpose: events and things no longer seem to occur by chance but rather are seen to have "underlying organization." The

seeker is able to intuit a deeper meaning beyond outer appearances and, importantly, something significant is revealed. William Meader explains beautifully below how to live life meaningfully is to participate in the consciousness of the soul.

When the soul is inwardly touched, a sense of purpose is slowly realized, and meaningful living then emerges in life. Meaning is therefore a state of consciousness. It represents an evolution away from perceiving outer events at face value. Instead, events are understood as symbols that reveal hidden significance. When a person begins to experience this, it indicates that s/he has stepped into the World of Meaning: the state of consciousness through which the soul's wisdom is revealed.
Meader 2013

Esoteric philosophy teaches that there are three aspects of mind: the lower concrete mind, the soul (son of mind) and the higher abstract mind. Situated within the abstract mind, the soul is the thinker and potentially has access to intuitional ways of knowing. The soul's primary task is to reorient consciousness towards those more subtle perceptions and the spiritual triad. In order for this to happen the soul must construct a bridge, or antahkarana, between itself and the spiritual triad, once the first stage of the bridging process is completed by the soul and personality. Consciousness is then able to function in two directions – towards the objective tangible world as well as the subjective inner world.

Antahkarana is a Sanskrit word: "antar" means interior or within and "karana" translates as sense organ. It is therefore defined as the inner organ or faculty and also known as the rainbow bridge. Esoterically, the antahkarana is described as a path or bridge between the lower and higher minds. To build the rainbow bridge, Alice

Bailey urged students to develop concentration through meditation or by simply focusing on any topic as concentration may be regarded as the first stage of meditation, the method par excellence to increase sensitivity to soul impression. Holistic education forerunner, Maria Montessori recognized that concentration produces an integration within a child's personality enabling the soul to shine forth.

According to *Messages from Kanchenjunga*, beauty (the likes of which is yet to be beheld) comprised of glorious currents of divine light, colour and celestial sound will set alight the soul, fanning it from a spark into a flame, in the coming age.

The "landscape" of the new world will ignite the spark of the soul into a flame through beauty of a magnitude now inconceivable. Waves of divine light raying forth in magnificent streams and bursts of colour, along with waves of celestial sound, will charge the "petals" of the crown chakra to open wider.
Messages from Kanchenjunga 2015, 10-11

In addition, the refinement of the colours and hues of your soul's "etheric garment" will signal to others your level of consciousness, destiny and purpose.

The soul will be clothed in a raiment of light that will identify, to the knowing onlooker, the level of consciousness attained over the course of lifetimes …. the etheric garment worn by each soul – woven of various rays of colour and hue, refinement and intensity – will signal to others a similarity or dissimilarity of destiny. Where there is mutual attraction there will be shared purpose. … In the world of the new age, all will be known by the quality of their light.
Messages from Kanchenjunga 2015, 23-24

So how may you, the seeker, become the knowing onlooker able to intuit the hidden meaning and significance of such "rays of colour and hue, refinement and intensity?" As the soul gains knowledge intuitively, subtle intuitive perceptions of this nature increasingly become possible as the antahkarana is constructed allowing subjective insights from the inner world of the soul, the world of meaning, to be consciously registered by your lower concrete mind. Wisdom, or true knowledge, ultimately resides within each individual.

Colour may be viewed as consciousness. From this perspective, the seven colours of the solar spectrum, each expressing a unique quality of light, are recognized as the outer reflection of inner forces emanating from the Seven Rays each of which: furnishes the soul and builds one of the seven kingdoms, rules one of the seven sacred planets, and provides the aura of one of the seven principles (the higher triad and lower quaternary) of a person with its colour.

In the following five brief statements (adapted), Helena Blavatsky explains how colour, the Seven Rays, the seven sacred planets and astrology are linked and relate to the soul.

1. Each of the Primordial Seven, the first Seven Rays forming the Manifested Logos, is again sevenfold.
2. As the seven colours of the solar spectrum correspond to the Seven Rays, or Hierarchies, so each of these latter has again its seven divisions corresponding to the same series of colours. One colour ... is predominant and more intense than the others.

> 3. Each of these Hierarchies furnishes the essence (the Soul) and is the "Builder" of one of the seven kingdoms of Nature which are the three elemental kingdoms, the mineral, the vegetable, the animal, and the kingdom of spiritual man.
> 4. Each Hierarchy furnishes the Aura of one of the seven principles in man with its specific colour.
> 5. Each of these Hierarchies is the Ruler of one of the Sacred Planets (thus) Astrology came into existence, and ... real Astrology has a strictly scientific basis.
> Blavatsky late 1800s, 481-82

The Seven Rays are a group of celestial Beings universally recognized as the seven Primeval Gods, or seven Hierarchies of Angels or Dhyan Chohans, referred to in Christian literature as the Seven Angels of the Presence. At the originating uppermost level of being, the Seven Rays are completely formless. As descent is made down into objectivity and form, they materialize more and more through every phase of existence – through humanity to the animal and plant kingdoms, then to the mineral kingdom where the descent finally ends. In accordance with occult teaching, Helena Blavatsky states that the purely spiritual group known as the Seven Rays is regarded as the nursery or fountain head of humanity. From them sprout that consciousness that is the "earliest manifestation from causal Consciousness – the Alpha and Omega of divine being and life forever" (Blavatsky late 1800s, 369).

A Circle is a Circle

The visible energy spectrum of the new humanity will include a breathtaking vista of colour and vibrancy at one end, a relative dimness at the other, and in between a panoply of varied textures and hues.
Messages from Kanchenjunga 2015, 6

In *The Secret Doctrine*, Helena Blavatsky describes the One, that all-pervading unity in which you live and move and have your being, as an unbroken, boundless circle that is nowhere and everywhere. Furthermore, within the circle are the vertical and horizontal, the father and mother. At the highest point of the wheel of life, the father connects with Spirit and at its base is form.

The One is an unbroken Circle (ring) with no circumference, for it is nowhere and everywhere; the One is the boundless plane of the Circle ... it is the Vertical and the Horizontal, the Father and the Mother, the summit and base of the Father, the two extremities of the Mother, reaching in reality nowhere, for the One is the Ring as also the rings that are within that Ring.
Blavatsky 1888, 11

Astrologically, Capricorn represents the father and Cancer the mother. Alice Bailey clearly links Capricorn and Cancer, located at either extremity of the zodiac wheel's vertical, with father – Spirit and mother – form.

It (Cancer) is allied with material nature, and with the mother of forms, just as the other gate, Capricorn, is allied with spirit, the father of all that IS.
Bailey 1951, 312

The zodiac wheel and colour wheel, ancient symbols of holism, unity and interconnectedness, are likewise represented by the boundless, unbroken circle symbolizing the One. In addition, these highly symbolic icons are both systematically divided into 12 equal sectors:

Colour Wheel ~ Red, Coral, Orange, Gold, Yellow, Olive Green, Green, Turquoise, Blue, Royal Blue, Violet, Deep Magenta.
Zodiac Wheel ~ Aries, Taurus, Gemini, Cancer, Leo, Virgo, Libra, Scorpio, Sagittarius, Capricorn, Aquarius, Pisces.

Colour Wheel

The traditional colour wheel used by artists and scientists today is attributed to Sir Isaac Newton who, about 300 years ago, developed a circular colour diagram that represented the visible spectrum of light after observing white light pass through a prism and diffract into seven colours. The three primary colours, Red, Yellow and Blue are placed equidistant around the colour wheel together with nine secondary and tertiary colours derived from them. Secondary colours, Orange, Green and Violet are formed by combining two primaries and are placed at the midway point between the two constituent colours. Tertiary colours, Coral, Gold, Olive Green, Turquoise, Royal Blue and Deep Magenta are formed by combining a primary and secondary and are placed directly between those two colours. Complementary colours (such as Yellow and Violet) are situated opposite each other on the colour wheel. The terms colour and hue are generally used interchangeably. Hue, however, refers to a dominant colour family and includes only one colour (for example Red or Blue) and shades of it.

In *Theory of Colours* (1810), Johann Wolfgang von Goethe linked colour categories with the emotional aspect of human functioning and since then colour psychology has fascinated many. Despite the fact that general research into colour's influence on psychological functioning is still emerging, colour psychology is hugely popular in marketing, performance, and art and design (Elliot 2015). When you learn about colour and your own personal colour code, you begin to recognize the "archetypal significance of colours, the universal meaning as well as culturally influenced nuances" (Booth and McKnight 2006, 13). Upon consideration, however, it's probably more likely a matter of remembering rather than learning or recognizing as, without exception, colour is one of the very first perceptions registered by the lower concrete mind of an infant or young child.

Based on intuitive cognition and understanding developed as an Aura-Soma practitioner, several key words are listed below for each of the 12 colours of the traditional colour wheel, offering a glimpse into their subtle nature or what they represent symbolically.

RED
Energy, passion, being grounded, material world, survival, non-attachment.

CORAL
Love wisdom, interconnectedness, cooperation, unrequited love.

ORANGE
Relationship, connection, shock, trauma, devotion, bliss.

GOLD
Inner wisdom, self-worth, purpose, joy, friendship, deep fear.

YELLOW
Happiness, confidence, understanding, knowledge, sunshine, the little will.

OLIVE GREEN
Feminine leadership, releasing bitterness from the heart, transmutation.

GREEN
The heart, truth, balance, harmony, change, feelings, space, time, nature.

TURQUOISE
Creativity, inner teacher, individuation, dolphins, crystals, technology.

BLUE
Communication, peace, trust, authority, nurturing, protection, Thy will.

ROYAL BLUE
Higher mind, intuition, vision, mystical, being alone.

VIOLET
Spirituality, service, transformation, loss, grief, healing.

DEEP MAGENTA
Rescue, the carer's carer, woundedness, the shadow, hidden.

Zodiac Wheel

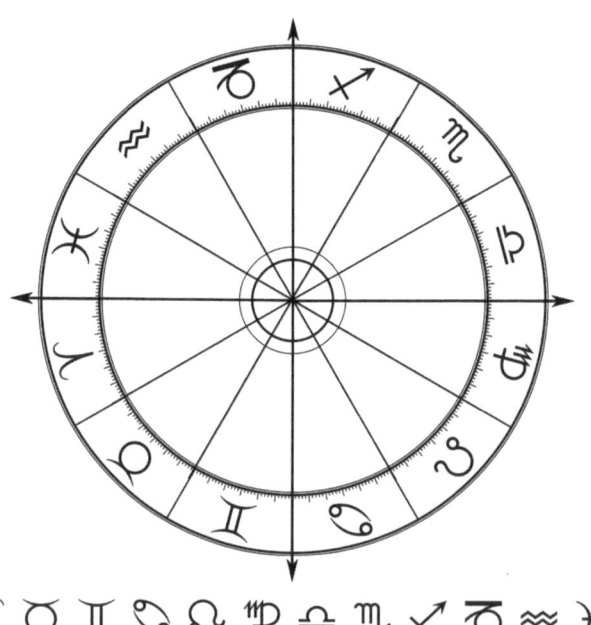

The zodiac wheel is comprised of 12 houses each occupied by one the 12 signs of the zodiac, constellations of stars that interact with each other forming great entities of being. Grouped together they function as intense energy centres expressing qualities such as love, power and self-expression.

The signs, in effect, give us the How a particular energy will be experienced. They colour the experience with the How.
Bayliss 2016, 12

According to esoteric astrologer Stephen Bayliss, the zodiac signs provide the "how" – how a particular energy is experienced – and they "colour" the experience with the how. Used in this sense, what idea does the term colour convey? Alice Bailey defines colour as the colour of light moving at different rates of vibration. In her view, the word colour reveals an intention as its definition implies the "idea of concealment." Colour is seen as an objective medium concealing an intention.

The very use of the word "Colour" shews the intention, for, as you know, the definition of the word conveys the idea of concealment. Colour is therefore "that which does conceal." It is simply the objective medium by means of which the inner force transmits itself; it is the reflection upon matter of the type of influence that is emanating from the Logos, and which has penetrated to the densest part of His solar system. We recognize it as colour.
Bailey 1950, 21

So what is it that colour conceals? Let's return to the zodiac wheel keeping in mind the notion that the zodiac signs colour the experience with the how. How is the particular energy of each zodiac sign experienced?

Alice Bailey's *exoteric* Words for the Signs of the Zodiac (1951, 653), expressing how each sign manifests in terms of form and matter in the three lower worlds (physical, emotional and mental), even though very brief, reveal a lot in this regard. These succinct statements describe the quality of the outward journey undertaken by the lower self, the personality, into the world of form – the very journey undertaken by the mass of people whose lives conform with recognized orthodox astrological conclusions.

When considering the exoteric Words for the Signs of the Zodiac, it's important to remember they describe the outward path of the personality – how the personality ray is expressed – around the zodiac wheel from the orthodox angle: from Aries to Taurus via Pisces and Aquarius. For this reason, zodiac signs (with planetary rulers as cited by Alice Bailey) are listed below in retrogressing order as per natural order according to the angle of form. As you shall see shortly, the seeker, having already experienced the crisis of reorientation, comes under other influences and therefore progresses around the zodiac wheel in reverse, from Aries to Pisces via Taurus and Gemini, expressing to the highest degree the qualities of her soul ray (Bailey 1951, 90-91).

Exoteric Words for Zodiac Signs

PISCES – JUPITER
And the Word said: Go forth into matter.

AQUARIUS – URANUS
And the Word said: Let desire in form be ruler.

CAPRICORN – SATURN
And the Word said: Let ambition rule and the door stand wide.

SAGITTARIUS – JUPITER
And the Word said: Let food be sought.

SCORPIO – MARS
And the Word said: Let Maya flourish and let deception rule.

LIBRA – VENUS
And the Word said: Let choice be made.

VIRGO – MERCURY
And the Word said: Let matter reign.

LEO – SUN
And the Word said: Let other forms exist. I rule.

CANCER – MOON
And the Word said: Let isolation be the rule and yet the crowd exists.

GEMINI – MERCURY
And the Word said: Let instability do its work.

TAURUS – VENUS
And the Word said: Let struggle be undismayed.

ARIES – MARS
And the Word said: Let form again be sought.

Esoteric Astrology

The conscious soul will sense the single Source of Life in the shifting, streaming waves of energy vibrating through subtle forms of endless varieties and intensities of light and colour.
Messages from Kanchenjunga 2015, 32

Traditional astrology posits one set of planetary rulers that the mass of humanity respond to. Esoteric astrology, concerned primarily with the unfoldment of consciousness, posits another set of esoteric rulers that the seeker, living through her chakras above the diaphragm, responds to (Bailey 1951, 65). The hidden purpose of your soul can be unveiled by esoteric astrology, a method of chart analysis that offers a deeper interpretation in relation to your spiritual life. In his *Emergent Light* blog, William Meader describes succinctly and beautifully how esoteric astrology seeks to understand the higher, purer qualities expressed by each zodiac sign and how it is able to reveal your soul's incarnational intention.

William Meader explains that spiritually the ascendant, or rising sign, governs the causal body, the abode of the soul or the form through which the soul functions; whereas in orthodox astrology the ascendant governs outer appearances and expression of the lower self. For this reason, in esoteric astrology the ascendant is crucial to understanding the soul's purpose and is therefore the most important sign when considering the chart of a person who consciously treads the path. Alice Bailey's description of this concept is clear and concise:

The sun sign ... indicates the present problem of the man; it sets the pace or the established tempo of his personality life ... the ascendant or rising sign indicates the intended life or immediate soul purpose for this incarnation. It holds the secret of the future and presents the force which, rightly used, will lead the man to success.
Bailey 1951, 18

The ascendant reveals the remote possibilities for soul development while the sun sign shows the more likely probabilities: development of the personality. Through a great transformational process, however, that slowly transpires over numerous lifetimes, the personality – the sun sign – eventually yields its authority to the soul – the ascendant – then acts as an effective instrument for it, the soul, to express itself creatively in service.

The moon represents the past and instinctual or unconscious tendencies which manifest in life as limitations, handicaps and obstacles that obstruct soul expression. William Meader sums up the powerful triangular relationship between the ascendant, sun and moon signs as follows:

When looking at these three signs we see an amazing transformational dynamic occurring. The ascendant conceals the hidden purpose of the Soul. To express this purpose successfully requires that the individual arrest the selfish tendencies engendered by the sun sign. This s/he does by nurturing the higher qualities offered by the sun sign. In addition, s/he must analyze the moon sign, and its negative tendencies, and discover ways of uplifting them. This is achieved by first becoming conscious

*of these tendencies, then finding ways of redirecting
them for the betterment of others.*
Meader 2013

The esoteric planetary rulers are regarded as the energetic representatives of the zodiac signs, symbolizing their higher traits. The ascendant's esoteric ruler is viewed as the ruling planet of the entire chart and reveals conditions for future spiritual growth; however, as awareness of your own soul increases, the influence of the planets weakens. Rather than the force of the planets themselves, the force flowing through the planets begins to govern and control. You then become receptive to the higher, subtler energies of the solar system and zodiacal constellations.

The effect of energies flowing through the 12 zodiac signs readies the seeker for the crisis of reorientation by means of which retrogression around the zodiac wheel is gradually reversed and the return journey back to source begun, patiently and consciously. Awakening proceeds and no longer are you affected by of the miasma of world maya. Reversal upon the wheel of life occurs and, slowly but surely, you begin to function as a soul struggling towards the light until you – the triumphant seeker – finally emerge at the end of the path in Pisces, typically fulfilling the role of a world saviour (Bailey 1951, 20-21).

As stated previously, the reversed zodiac wheel progresses from Aries to Pisces via Taurus and Gemini – instead of from Aries to Taurus via Pisces and Aquarius. Occult rumour purports that once upon the reversed wheel the seeker experiences exactly 12 incarnations, one in each of the 12 zodiac signs, wherein great moments of crisis occur necessitating she prove herself spiritually until detachment from form is eventually achieved – enabling complete freedom from the wheel of rebirth (Bailey 1951, 83).

Orthodox planets are concerned with the physical plane expression of the personality whereas zodiac signs are concerned primarily with the stimulation of the soul, producing subjective awareness and, in turn, changes in outer expression (Bailey 1951, 52). Such profound changes are achieved through the blending of the energy of each constellation with the energy of the planets. Alice Bailey (1951, 23) states that the "disciple has to become consciously aware of the planetary influences and begin to use them for the carrying out of soul purpose ... the initiate has to be aware of the zodiacal influences which emanate from outside of the solar system" – and these may be recognized as a vibration in one of the seven chakras, the revelation of a particular type of light conveying a specific colour, or a peculiar note or sound.

When considering the chart of a person who seeks to consciously tread the path, it's crucial to use the Seven Rays as an interpretative tool especially in relation to the ascendant and sun sign. This subject may seem complex, however, in truth, the Seven Rays are comprised of the most fundamental qualities in existence within the cosmos. Each Ray conditions humanity with a different quality of Spirit – as their names and words of power imply. The originating source of the Seven Rays are the seven stars of the constellation known as the Great Bear or Big Dipper (two come from Sirius and three from the Pleiades) transmitted to Earth through the seven stars of the Little Bear. The seven Rishis of the Great Bear express themselves through seven planetary Logoi that manifest through the seven sacred planets: Vulcan, Mercury, Venus, Jupiter, Saturn, Neptune and Uranus.

The Seven Rays enter our solar system via the 12 zodiac signs, revealing the highest qualities seeking expression through each constellation. Each Ray conveys itself through three zodiac signs, however, some signs radiate one Ray while others radiate two or three (Bailey

1951, 85-86). The table below shows the triplicity of zodiac signs and planetary rulers (cited as per Alice Bailey) utilized by each of these seven great streams of energy to transmit their force to Earth.

The Seven Rays

Ray	Zodiac Signs	Exoteric Rulers	Esoteric Rulers
Ray 1 Divine Will or Power	Aries Leo Capricorn	Mars Sun Saturn	Mercury Sun Saturn
Ray 2 Love Wisdom	Gemini Virgo Pisces	Mercury Mercury Jupiter	Venus Moon Pluto
Ray 3 Active Intelligence	Cancer Libra Capricorn	Moon Venus Saturn	Neptune Uranus Saturn
Ray 4 Harmony Through Conflict	Taurus Scorpio Sagittarius	Venus Mars Jupiter	Vulcan Mars Earth
Ray 5 Concrete Knowledge	Leo Sagittarius Aquarius	Sun Jupiter Uranus	Sun Earth Jupiter
Ray 6 Idealism or Devotion	Virgo Sagittarius Pisces	Mercury Jupiter Jupiter	Moon Earth Pluto
Ray 7 Ceremonial Order	Aries Cancer Capricorn	Mars Moon Saturn	Mercury Neptune Saturn

This cosmic transmission process – how each of the Seven Rays makes its way from the Great Bear to Earth via three zodiacal constellations and their ruling planets – is depicted over the next seven pages in adapted versions of Alice Bailey's Diagram 4 (Bailey 1951, 610-11). The key for the transmission of each Ray's energy is summed up in four terms:

Transcending ~ The Seven Rays are the transcending cause.
Transmitting ~ Three zodiac signs act as transmitting agents of forces emitted by each Ray.
Transforming ~ Quality of forces bettered as they pass through transforming agent, the Sun (or soul).
Transfiguring ~ Transfiguration process gradually converts non-sacred planets into sacred planets.

In the following Ray diagrams only four of the five non-sacred planets are listed as Earth is one of them. The Sun and Moon are viewed as non-sacred planets as, in this instance, they act as blinds or veils. For further clarification, the breakdown of sacred and non-sacred planets and each planet's particular Ray is tabulated below.

Planets & Rays

Sacred Planet	*Non-Sacred Planet*	*Ray*
Vulcan	Pluto	Ray 1
Jupiter	Sun (hidden planet)	Ray 2
Saturn	Earth	Ray 3
Mercury	Moon (hidden planet)	Ray 4
Venus		Ray 5
Neptune	Mars	Ray 6
Uranus		Ray 7

First Ray of Will or Power

I assert the fact.

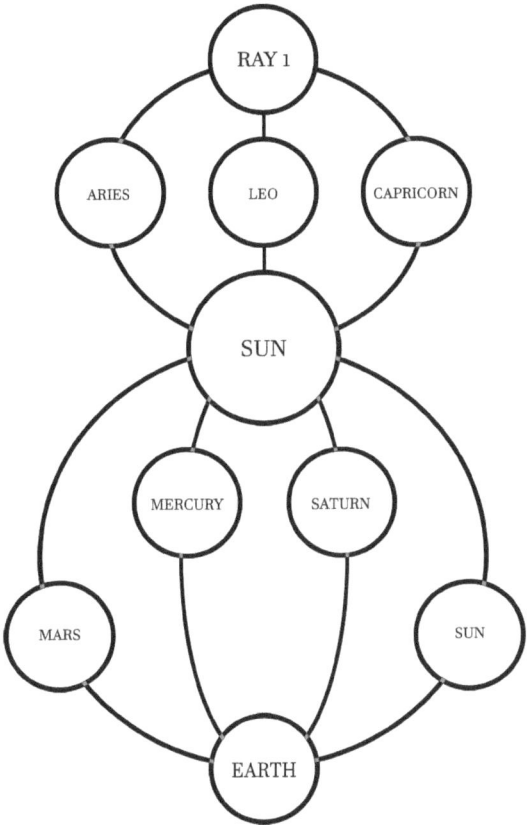

Zodiac Signs: Aries, Leo & Capricorn
Sacred Planets: Mercury & Saturn
Non-Sacred Planets: Mars & Sun

Natural born leaders belong to the Ray of Will or Power, either wholly or in part. Ray 1 approaches the path by sheer force of will or, as it has been said, takes the kingdom of heaven by storm.

Second Ray of Love Wisdom

I see the greatest light.

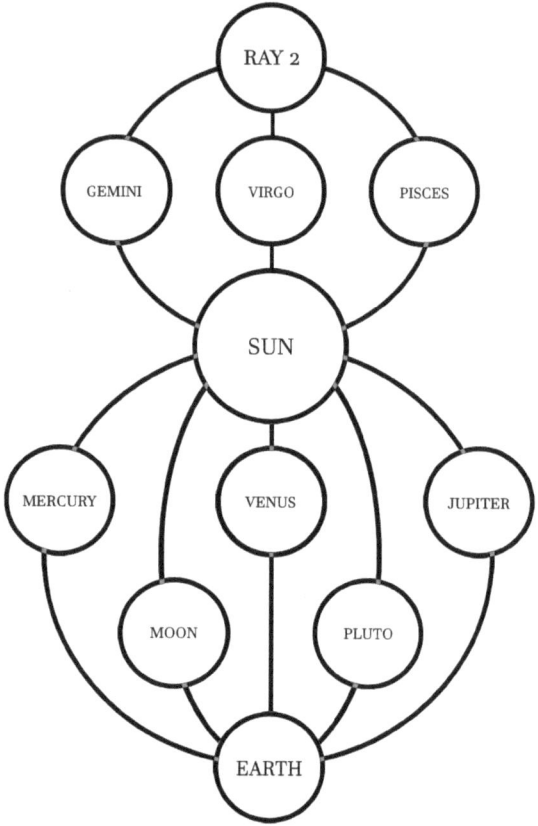

Zodiac Signs: Gemini, Virgo & Pisces
Sacred Planets: Mercury, Venus & Jupiter
Non-Sacred Planets: Moon & Pluto

Ray 2 studies the teachings diligently until they become a spiritual rule of living instead of being perceived as mere intellectual knowledge. The intuition and true wisdom are thus brought in.

Third Ray of Abstract Intelligence & Activity

Purpose itself am I.

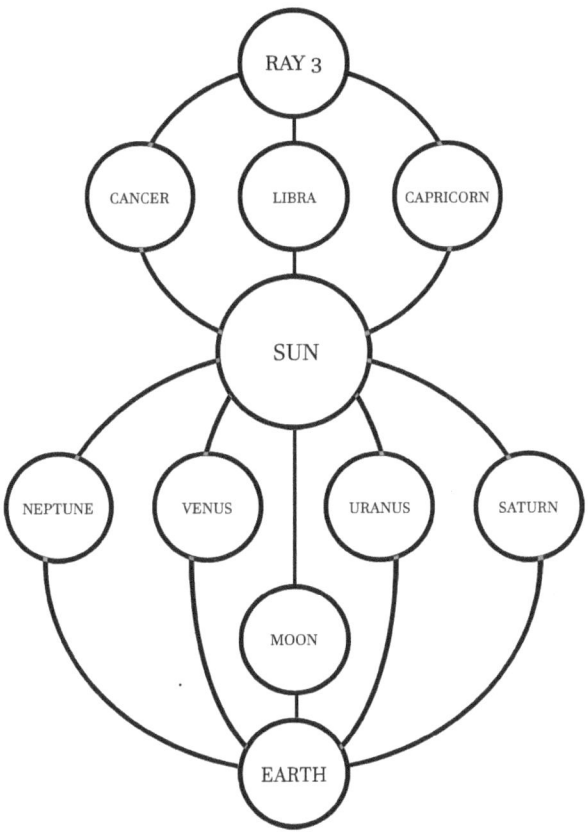

*Zodiac Signs: Cancer, Libra & Capricorn
Sacred Planets: Neptune, Venus, Uranus & Saturn
Non-Sacred Planet: Moon*

The Ray of the higher mind and abstract thinker, Ray 3 thinks deeply on philosophic or metaphysical topics – until realization of the importance of treading the path and of the "great beyond" leads her there.

Fourth Ray of Harmony Through Conflict

Two merge with One.

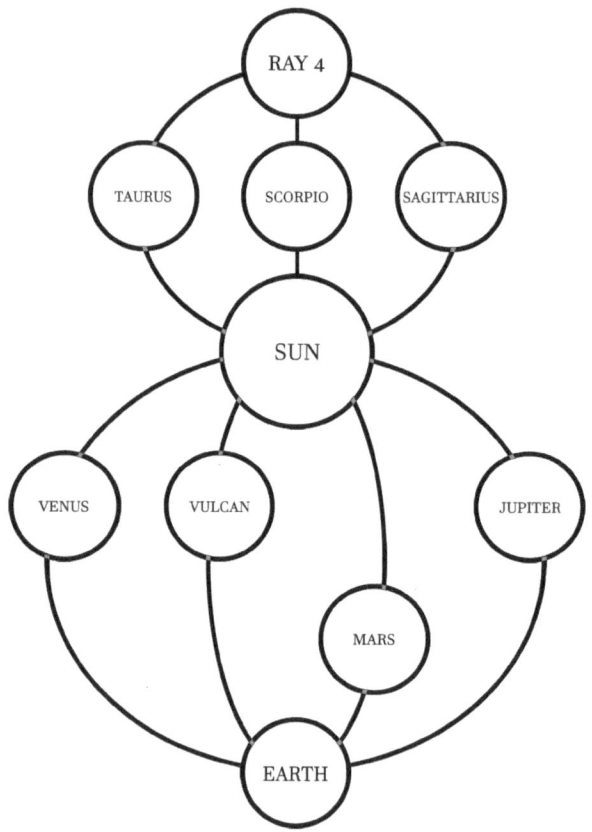

Zodiac Signs: Taurus, Scorpio & Sagittarius
Sacred Planets: Venus, Vulcan & Jupiter
Non-Sacred Planet: Mars

Ray 4, the Ray of struggle, approaches the path through self-control. Equilibrium between the warring forces of activity and inertia is cultivated as well as mental and moral balance.

Fifth Ray of Concrete Knowledge

Three minds unite.

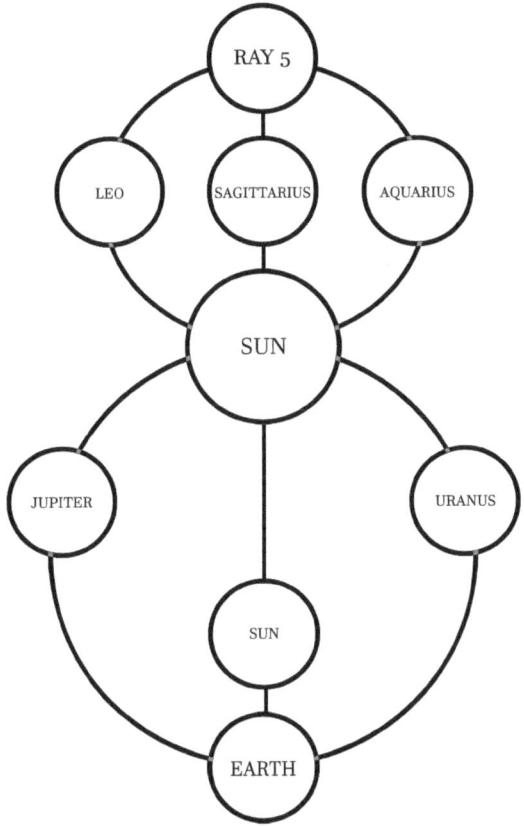

Zodiac Signs: Leo, Sagittarius & Aquarius
Sacred Planets: Jupiter & Uranus
Non-Sacred Planet: Sun

The Ray of the lower mind, Ray 5 approaches the path through scientific research – tracing facts to their source, coming to ultimate conclusions and accepting the inferences that follow.

Sixth Ray of Idealism or Devotion

The highest light controls.

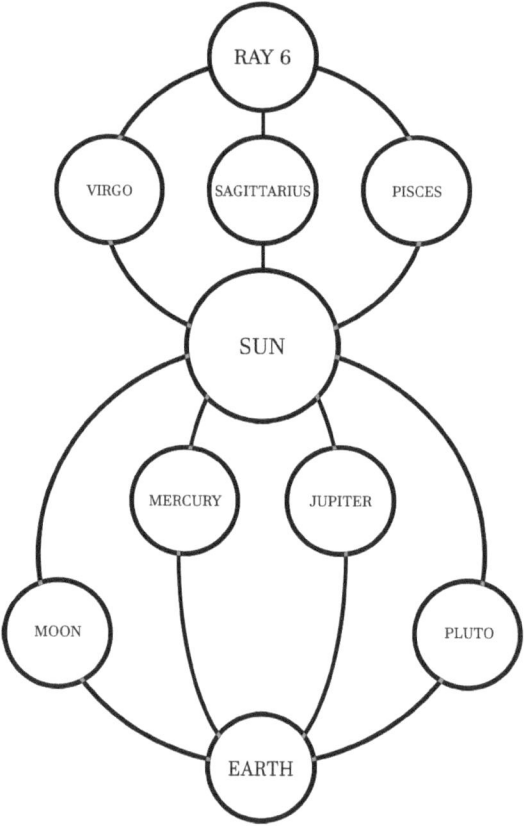

Zodiac Signs: Virgo, Sagittarius & Pisces
Sacred Planets: Mercury & Jupiter
Non-Sacred Planets: Moon & Pluto

Prayer and meditation seeking union with God are methods used to approach the path. Full of religious instincts, impulses and intense personal feelings, Ray 6 aspires to be tolerant, serene and balanced.

Seventh Ray of Ceremonial Order

The highest and lowest meet.

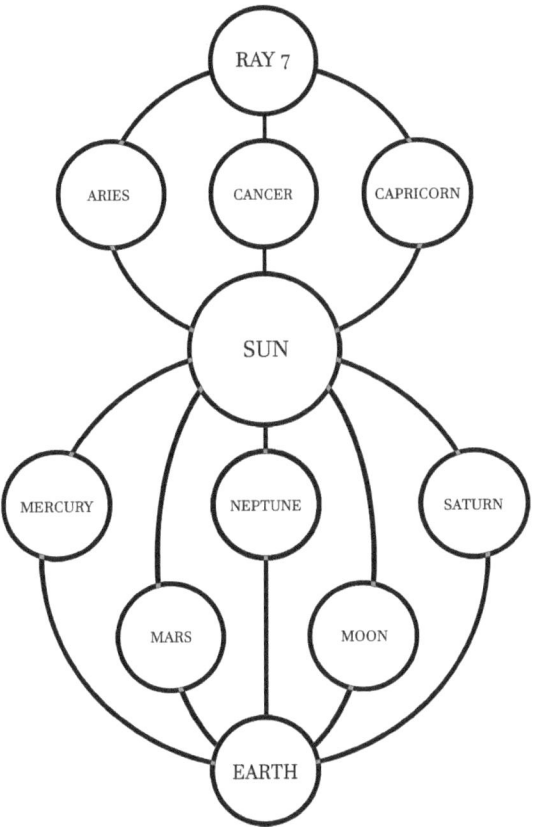

Zodiac Signs: Aries, Cancer & Capricorn
Sacred Planets: Mercury, Neptune & Saturn
Non-Sacred Planets: Mars & Moon

The path is approached through ritual and observance of the rules of practice. The elemental forces are easily evoked and controlled on Ray 7, the Ray of ceremony, magic and form.

Colour & Astrology

To listen to the song of the sparrow or the dove is to hear a discrete manifestation of the Life that infuses all of creation with Itself. Likewise, to notice the textures, colours and shapes of the daffodil and the hyacinth is to recognize singular imprints of the Creator.
Messages from Kanchenjunga 2015, 32

Imagine a colour wheel and zodiac wheel, one stacked on top of the other, with Red and Aries, the first house, placed together. With Red and Aries so aligned, within each of these ancient, universal symbols – both based on the circle – are the vertical and horizontal.

Residing at the summit of the vertical of the colour wheel is intuitive Royal Blue representing inner vision and the higher mind; and at its base is Gold, where the incarnational star signifies wisdom at the deepest point of being. At the two extremities of the colour wheel's horizontal are colours that form a continuum between the physical and emotional worlds: Red, symbolizing manifestation, survival in the physical world, and material things such as wealth and possessions; and harmonious Green – the heart, the seeker, the way, the truth and the life.

At the highest point of the zodiac wheel's vertical, on the cusp of the tenth house sits the midheaven where Capricorn, the sign of initiation, depicts the setting for the uppermost projection of the personality in terms of capabilities, qualities and achievement. At the base of the vertical on the fourth house cusp is Cancer, traditionally ruled by the Moon, representing the feminine, home and emotional life. This angle, known as the nadir, is the transformation point of a chart which marks the accumulation of impressions from the past that show what you truly are (Evans 1979, 40). At either extremity of the zodiac wheel's horizontal are the ascendant (pertaining to self) on the first house cusp; and Libra, seventh house of justice, relationship and balance (pertaining to others). Revealing the focus in life – either outer or inner – the horizontal and vertical of the zodiac wheel act as doorways into the respective spheres of the four angular houses, each tenanted by cardinal signs and characterized by initiative, focus and action.

Zodiac Colour Wheel

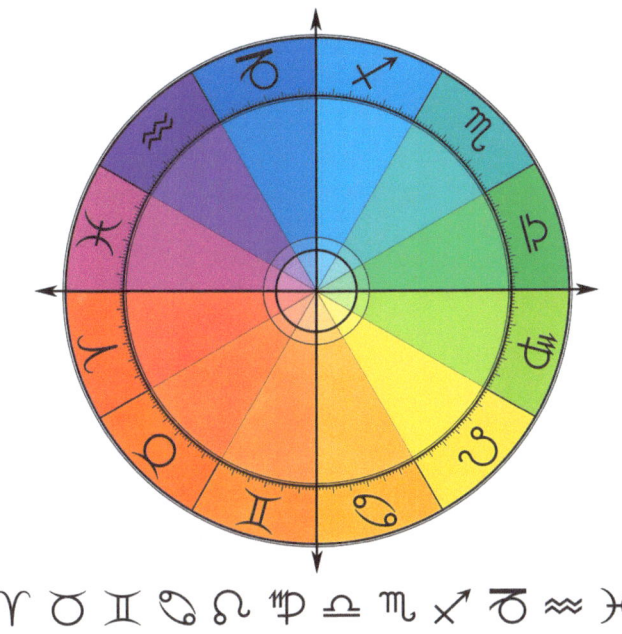

Aries Taurus Gemini Cancer Leo Virgo Libra Scorpio Sagittarius Capricorn Aquarius Pisces

Below, the 12 zodiac signs are coupled with the colours they link with when these two iconic wheels, which seem to share a vast sum of interwoven symbology, are so aligned. Beneath each pairing are Alice Bailey's *esoteric Words for the Signs of the Zodiac* (1951, 653-54), short statements that eloquently describe each constellation's higher, purer qualities as experienced by the soul upon the return path; and esoteric planetary rulers – the planets that the seeker, living through her chakras above the diaphragm, responds to. Zodiac signs are listed in spiritual order – the correct order from the angle of the soul.

Esoteric Words for Zodiac Signs

RED/ARIES – MERCURY
I come forth and from the plane of mind I rule.

CORAL/TAURUS – VULCAN
I see, and when the eye is opened, all is illumined.

ORANGE/GEMINI – VENUS
I recognize my other self and in the waning of that self I grow and glow.

GOLD/CANCER – NEPTUNE
I build a lighted house and therein dwell.

YELLOW/LEO – SUN
I am That and That am I.

OLIVE GREEN/VIRGO – MOON VEILING VULCAN
I am the Mother and the Child. I, God, I matter am.

GREEN/LIBRA – URANUS
I choose the way that leads between the two great lines of force.

TURQUOISE/SCORPIO – MARS
Warrior I am, and from the battle I emerge triumphant.

BLUE/SAGITTARIUS – EARTH
I see the goal. I reach the goal and see another.

ROYAL BLUE/CAPRICORN – SATURN
Lost am I in light supernal, yet on that light I turn my back.

VIOLET/AQUARIUS – JUPITER
Water of life am I, poured forth for thirsty men.

DEEP MAGENTA/PISCES – PLUTO
I leave the Father's Home and turning back, I save.

Of special interest are the parallels – shared qualities and characteristics – which are evident when symbology associated with the colour wheel and astrological symbolism of the zodiac wheel is compared. An evaluation of some connections between each colour and its corresponding sign is set out below. The colour key words, ruling planet traits and esoteric Words for the Signs of the Zodiac form the basis of these brief interpretations. I urge you to ponder the nature of the common threads linking each colour and zodiac sign, as through contemplation the wisdom of the soul may be recognized in consciousness.

Red/Aries

Red, representing dynamic energy, manifestation and being safely and securely grounded in the physical world, joins with Aries where purification is achieved as the result of war and strife through the influence of fiery Mars. Mercury enables the seeker in Aries, the birthplace of ideas, to comprehend the divine plan underlying those battleground experiences.

Coral/Taurus

Taurus struggles to break the illusive hold of selfish desire until the light of revelation breaks through transmuting desire into aspiration and blindness into vision. Self-pity, the effect of concentrating on frustrated desires, is succeeded by the group conscious Coral attributes of love wisdom, cooperation and collaboration as well as recognizing and cooperating with the divine plan.

Orange/Gemini

Orange and Mercury, Gemini's traditional ruler, are both concerned with relationship and the etheric body. Gemini governs relationship between the pair of opposites, keeping relations fluid as duality must eventually become one. Likewise, Orange restores wholeness to the etheric body following shock and trauma. Acting as an intermediary between the soul and physical body, the etheric body eventually becomes the transmitter of soul energy. When recognized, the personality begins to wane and the soul increasingly shines forth. Orange, the colour of devotion, connection and bliss, links with Gemini, governed esoterically by Venus, where duality is resolved through love.

Gold/Cancer

At the deepest point of an individual, within the Gold area, lies the incarnational star. Similarly, Cancer, governing home and the emotions, resides at the deepest point of the zodiac wheel. Cancer's focused energy creates a magnetic point that leads to the incarnation of the soul; its innate sensitivity is needed to develop wisdom and cooperation with the divine plan. Resonating with the soul's very essence is the wisdom of Gold, especially with regard to its relationship with form.

Yellow/Leo

Yellow, positive, happy and alert, denotes acquired knowledge, understanding and the little will. Leo, too, is concerned with the intellect or mind. Driven by an intrinsic urge towards self-knowledge, mental perception and intellectual positivity, Leo is the dominantly self-aware sign that can remain uninfluenced and in control. The desire to seek control and to rule leads Leo and Yellow to self-mastery and control of the personality, fuelled by motives either selfish or altruistic.

Olive Green/Virgo

Esoterically, the Moon (veiling Vulcan) rules Virgo, the cosmic mother who represents receptivity. Vulcan signifies persistence, endurance and continuity of effort. Virgo guards, nourishes and hides the Christ child within herself; and is the "womb of time" in which the divine plan is slowly matured through pain, discomfort, struggle and conflict symbolized by very deep, dark, prolonged crises that eventually lead to light. Similarly, the Olive Green process of transmutation gradually releases bitterness from the heart transmuting it into freedom, hope and the ability to advocate on behalf of others – through engaging the feminine, intuitive nature in a proactive manner.

Green/Libra

Truth and balance are key for both Libra and Green. Resonating with the harmony and tranquility of Green, the heart chakra is situated at the midway point between the three higher and three lower chakras. By the time the seeker steps onto the path, the three higher chakras are functioning to varying degrees, whereas life for the majority is experienced through the lower chakras. Libra seeks balance at the midway point between the constantly fluctuating pair of opposites: personal desire and spiritual love. The interlude when equilibrium is attained between the material and spiritual law proffers situations and opportunities involving typical Green scenarios – such as crossroads, choices being made and new directions.

Turquoise/Scorpio

Esoterically, Mars (often associated with Red, the complement of Turquoise on the RGB colour wheel) rules Scorpio – whose watery, emotional nature provides the perfect setting for Turquoise to express itself creatively from the heart. In Scorpio, memory and imagination act as creative agents enabling Turquoise's creativity to unfold. The sign of test, trial and triumph, Scorpio influences the turning point. Old identifications cease making way for more subtle, higher ones: spiritual imagination replaces glamour, the personality is subdued and ambition replaced by soul expression.

Blue/Sagittarius

The "blue planet" Earth is the esoteric ruler of Sagittarius which links with the colour Blue, indicative of trust, protective strength and direction. One-pointed spiritual aspiration drives the seeker in Sagittarius who tends to aim for a goal then refocuses towards a higher one whilst developing a basic, directing purpose. Symbolically, the Sagittarian archer focuses the arrow of her mind unwaveringly on the objective sought. Blue relates to the throat chakra used on the return path to create in a higher, spiritual sense: to communicate peacefully, to nurture others, and to express love wisdom dedicated to the betterment of Earth – the planet of struggle, pain and sorrow – and her inhabitants.

Royal Blue/Capricorn

Royal Blue connects with the third eye chakra, the intuition and higher mind. Saturn, restrictor and bearer of struggle and responsibility, resonates with the Royal Blue qualities of solitude, being alone and loneliness. Representing the father aspect and most material of all signs, Capricorn offers full expression of the earthly nature and immense spiritual possibilities. With the midheaven sitting on its cusp, Capricorn signifies the mountain top, the pinnacle of achievement and conclusion, where Royal Blue's inner vision is attained opening the door to the life of Spirit.

Violet/Aquarius

Like Aquarius, Violet serves, heals and transforms. In Aquarius, service of the lower self is transformed into service of humanity: superficial, selfish living is transformed into a deep, active intention to serve and a sensitive humanitarian awareness. Symbolically, the Aquarian water bearer stores all she has for service in her water pot giving it out freely on demand to meet need as and when required. Uranus, the liberator, bestows spontaneous activity producing constant movement and evolutionary development. Consecrated to service and the welfare of others, Violet and Aquarius dispense spirituality to humanity.

Deep Magenta/Pisces

Pisces' sensitivity, detachment from form and regeneration are reflected in Deep Magenta's resonance with divine love, attention to the little things and the restoration of wholeness. In Pisces, the personality finally succumbs making way for the release of the soul from its

imprisoning form. Demonstrating the Piscean qualities of devotion and response to the needs of humanity, the soul is able to return to the task of world saviour. Pisces and Deep Magenta make use of their characteristic mental sensitivity, compassionate nature and spiritual awareness to rescue themselves and others – making them whole, well and complete.

Whilst I am not an Aura-Soma teacher, I would like to take this opportunity to offer a suggestion for fellow practitioners that may help when considering an Aura-Soma Equilibrium selection. As practitioners are aware, the upper fraction of an Equilibrium bottle represents the conscious, what is happening in the outer, physical world or the personality whereas the lower fraction denotes the unconscious, the inner potential or the soul. I must reiterate that this is not in accordance with Aura-Soma's current methodology; however, I find that intuitively relating Alice Bailey's exoteric and/or esoteric Words for the Signs of the Zodiac to each colour chosen, carefully noting where each colour is situated – in either the upper (exoteric) or lower (esoteric) fraction as well as its position within the overall selection – helps to provide a subtle, deeply insightful additional layer of meaning.

Beloved principal of ASIACT, Mike Booth makes a clear distinction between the outward and return paths in his Aura-Soma teachings. The former involves the outward tendency of the personality into the world of form and matter – and the latter, once the turning point is reached, consists of the return journey back into the formless world of the soul, the world of meaning. In connection with these deeply symbolic paths, within the

Aura-Soma colour care system, Equilibrium bottles 0 to 21 comprise the outward set and corresponding bottles 22 and 79 to 99 make up the return set. When these particular Equilibrium bottles are selected, may I also suggest it may assist to once again intuitively relate Alice Bailey's exoteric and/or esoteric Words for the Signs of the Zodiac to the colours chosen, mindfully discerning the different orientation between bottles belonging to the outward (exoteric) and return (esoteric) sets.

Finally, set out on the following pages are symbolic key words for each of the 15 colours included in the Aura-Soma colour care system and affirmations that aspire to support the growth of each colour's higher, purer qualities. Whether these provide an insight into an Equilibrium bottle you are using, if they help in colour consultations or you share them with students, if they simply help you to better understand the colours you are drawn to – or the significance of ordinary and extraordinary colour based experiences and things that appear in daily life – it is my sincere hope that your life may be enriched meaningfully and purposefully by your enlightened understanding of the sacred language of colour.

Colour Key Words

Have you ever heard the celestial music of the spheres? Have you ever listened to the flapping of an insect's wings? Have you ever noticed the magenta of a perfect sunset?
We pose these questions to evoke greater sensitivity to the refinement of Our world, where nothing of the denser planes remains except the light distilled from passing through them.
Messages from Kanchenjunga 2015, 26

White

LIGHT, PURITY, INTENSITY, THE WELL OF UNSHED TEARS, ENLIGHTENMENT

Illumination, karmic absolution; clarity, need for clarity; clearing, clear, unclear; transparent, shining, reflecting; light at the end of the tunnel, blinded by the light; all colours; united, unity; adaptable, flexible; scattered, messy; tears, suffering, anguish, yearning; all seems magnified, emotionally overloaded or lost; weighed down, light as a feather; emotional vacuum, blank, withdrawn; deluded; icy, frosty, frozen inside; hazy, foggy, dull; no lustre, light, shine or sparkle.

I shine the light of my soul on all I think, feel and do.

AFFIRMATION: I am a beacon of light illuminating the way of my brothers and sisters on the path.

Pink

UNCONDITIONAL LOVE, ACCEPTANCE, SELF-LOVE, WARMTH, CARING

Feminine, awakened heart; being kind, thoughtful; gentle, soft, tender, timid; fragile, vulnerable, strong; accepting or not accepting self; loving or not loving self; longing for love, surrendering to love, letting love in; feeling loved, unloved or hurt; love addiction, love-struck; sensitive, perceptive, reading between the lines; caring, not caring, listening, not listening; feeling heard or unheard, wanted or unwanted; manipulating, demanding; hidden anger, resentment or frustration; intense red issues.

I love all parts of myself unconditionally.

AFFIRMATION: I stand at the centre of love and from there move outward.

Red

ENERGY, PASSION, MATERIAL WORLD, BEING GROUNDED, SURVIVAL, NON-ATTACHMENT

Sacrificial love; awakened, instinctive; life, blood; feeling safe and securely grounded; energetic, passionate, enthusiastic; dynamic, powerful; hurried, impatient, frustrated, driven; hyperactive, frantic, manic; powerless, depleted, jaded, tired; exhausted, zapped, flat, inert; resentment, anger, conflict; offence, offending; threatening, attacking, reacting; heated, fuming, furious; cantankerous, hostile, aggressive; explosive, outrage; cashed up, broke; beaten, destitute; Earth star.

I let go with love.

ARIES

FORM: Let form again be sought.
SOUL: I come forth and from the plane of mind I rule.

Coral
**INTERCONNECTEDNESS, COOPERATION,
LOVE WISDOM, UNREQUITED LOVE**

New Christ consciousness, group or collective consciousness, the greater good; loving wisely, releasing expectations in relationships, considering the needs of others and the environment; impersonal; sensitive, tough outside but soft inside; selfish, unselfish; cooperative, uncooperative; collaboration, teamwork; community, network; interdependent, mutually supporting; hidden, undeclared or unreciprocated love.

Considering the greater good, I love wisely.

TAURUS
FORM: Let struggle be undismayed.
SOUL: I see, and when the eye is opened, all is illumined.

Orange
**RELATIONSHIP, CONNECTION, DEVOTION,
SHOCK, TRAUMA, BLISS**

Sociable, gregarious; sensual, sexual; devoted, committed, staunch; aspiring, celebrating; elated, rapture, ecstasy, deep joy; uncertainty, distress; devastated, traumatized; shocked, shattered, broken; put broken pieces together again; clearing conditioned patterns, healing the timeline; insightful, etheric; connected, disconnected; association, disassociation; functional, dysfunctional; dependent, independent, codependent.

I grow and glow with deep joy.

GEMINI
FORM: Let instability do its work.
SOUL: I recognize my other self and in the waning of that self I grow and glow.

Gold

INNER WISDOM, SELF-WORTH, PURPOSE, JOY, DEEP FEAR, FRIENDSHIP

Wisdom, realization, innate knowing, gut feelings; deep happiness, exaltation, joyfulness, delight; achievement, recognition; true friends; life purpose, living a purposeful and meaningful life; judging or not judging; feeling worthy or unworthy, valued or not valued; underrated or overrated, adequate or inadequate; self-doubt, insecurities, irrational fears, deep confusion; high or low self-esteem; the incarnational star.

I am centred and present.

CANCER
FORM: Let isolation be the rule and yet the crowd exists.
SOUL: I build a lighted house and therein dwell.

Yellow

HAPPINESS, KNOWLEDGE, UNDERSTANDING, CONFIDENCE, FEAR, THE LITTLE WILL

Lightness, sunshine; smiles, laughter; happy, unhappy, smiles but unhappy inside; self-assurance, poise; mentally alert or drained; accurate, sharp, brilliant; stretched, stressed, frazzled; highly strung, nervous laughter; anxious, fearful, tense; apprehensive, concerned, worried; certain, uncertain; confused, bewildered; scared, frightened, intimidated, afraid; being brave or courageous; in or out of control, controlling or being controlled; procrastinating, assimilating, completing.

I choose love, not fear.

LEO
FORM: Let other forms exist. I rule.
SOUL: I am That and That am I.

Olive Green

TRANSMUTATION, FEMININE LEADERSHIP, RELEASING BITTERNESS FROM THE HEART

Feminine intuition; female leadership of the heart, the joy of making space for yourself and others; optimism, gratitude, appreciation; feeling hopeful, giving hope to others, advocating; freedom from bitterness and fear; surrendering, liberating, freeing; negativity, disappointment, betrayal; feeling pessimistic, gloomy or hopeless, expecting the worse.

In touch with my feminine intuitive side, I lead with my heart.

VIRGO

FORM: Let matter reign.
SOUL: I am the Mother and the Child. I, God, I matter am.

Green

THE HEART, TRUTH, FEELINGS, HARMONY, BALANCE, CHANGE, SPACE, TIME, NATURE

Balanced, unbalanced; equilibrium, tranquility, serenity; honesty, integrity; living your truth; honouring self, self-betrayal; an open, loving heart; closed, hurt or broken heart; overwhelmed by emotions or none at all; direct, frank, blunt; envy, jealousy; decisions, crossroads, new beginnings; searching, seeking; remembering, forgetting; feeling lost, cramped, squashed, stuck, trapped, spaced out; seeing the "big picture," can't see forest for the trees.

I honour the truth of my heart.

LIBRA

FORM: Let choice be made.
SOUL: I choose the way that leads between the two great lines of force.

Turquoise

CREATIVITY, INNER TEACHER, INDIVIDUATION, DOLPHINS, CRYSTALS, TECHNOLOGY

Idealistic, humanitarian; creative, imaginative, artistic; tech-savvy, technophobic; communicating from one to many; mass media, mass culture, mass hysteria; the collective unconscious; creative communication from the heart and feeling side of being; the ability or inability to express feelings; creative flow, creativity block; fluid, need for fluidity, going with the flow; playfulness, wanting or having fun; "fluffiness," overindulging, doing to excess.

I listen to the small, still voice within.

SCORPIO
FORM: Let Maya flourish and let deception rule.
SOUL: Warrior I am, and from the battle I emerge triumphant.

Blue

COMMUNICATION, PEACE, NURTURING, PROTECTION, AUTHORITY, TRUST, THY WILL

Masculine, male role model; nurturing mother, protective or problematic father; authority figures, owning your inner authority; trusting, distrusting, being trustworthy; peaceful, calm, content; communicating peacefully; finding your voice, speaking up; pensive, expressive, fluent; gift of the gab, chatterbox, loud; tongue-tied, reticent; shy, reserved; quiet, silent; distant, cold; dejected, despondent, depressed; introvert, extrovert.

I focus on inner peace, and trust. All is well.

SAGITTARIUS
FORM: Let food be sought.
SOUL: I see the goal. I reach the goal and see another.

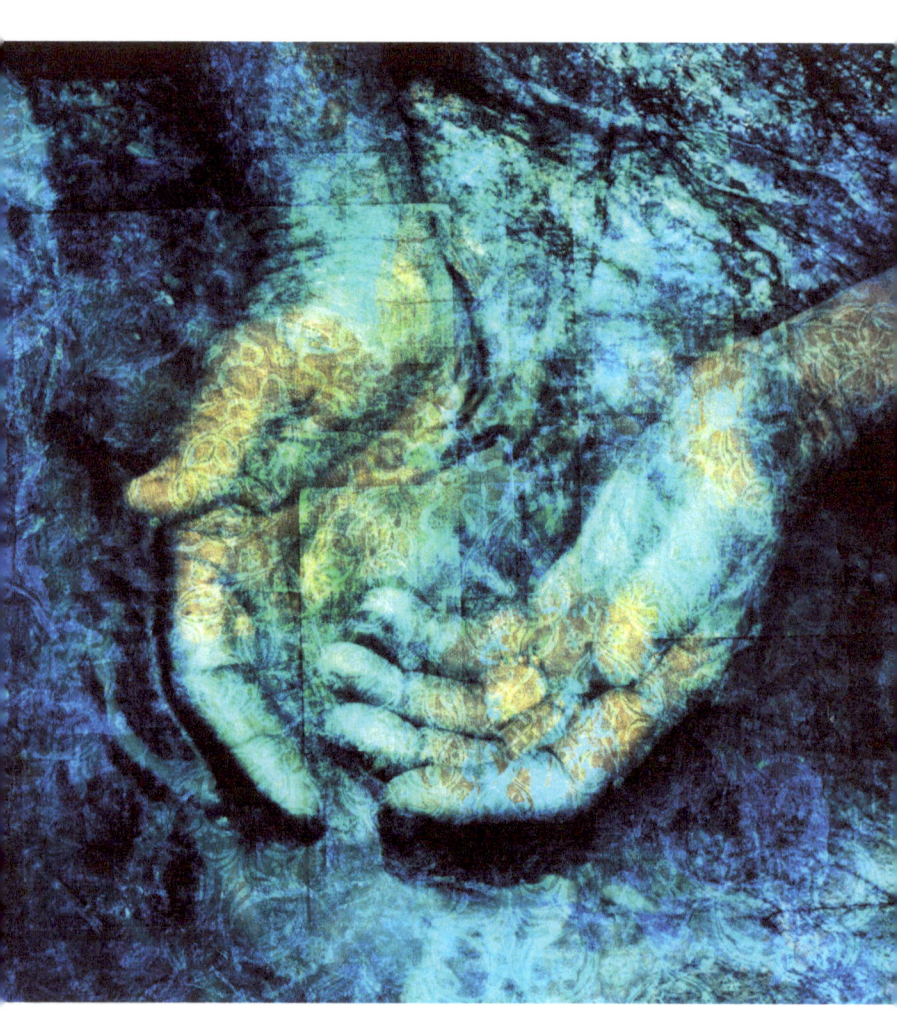

Royal Blue

HIGHER MIND FUNCTIONS, INTUITION, VISION, MYSTICAL, BEING ALONE

Clairvoyant, clairaudient, clairsentient; recognizing and trusting inner perceptions; inner vision, hearing and feeling; perceiving, visualizing, envisioning; thinking abstractly, intuitive understanding; stillness, intention, expertise; inspired, inspiring, inspiration; aloneness, solitude; seclusion, isolation; feeling lonely, alone in a crowd or misunderstood; rigidity, aloofness; big communication and authority issues.

I see, hear and feel clearly within.

CAPRICORN

FORM: Let ambition rule and the door stand wide.
SOUL: Lost am I in light supernal, yet on that light I turn my back.

Violet

SPIRITUALITY, SERVICE, TRANSFORMATION, LOSS, GRIEF, HEALING

A catalyst; helping others; dedicated, humble, spiritual; seeking perfection; kindred spirits, sharing, feeling uplifted; meditating, contemplating; grieving, mourning, missing people, pets or situations; empty, vague, remote, out of it; removed from what's going on, not grounded; in head too much, get head together; physical, emotional or spiritual healing; feeling superior or inferior, better or worse off; self-pity, wanting to escape or go "home."

Giving freely, I serve.

AQUARIUS

FORM: Let desire in form be ruler.
SOUL: Water of life am I, poured forth for thirsty men.

Deep Magenta

RESCUE, THE CARER'S CARER, WOUNDEDNESS, THE SHADOW, HIDDEN

Divine love within the depths; great potential, the potential of all things; absorbs all colours; replenishing, renewing, restoring; making whole again; saving, rescuing, compulsive rescuing; giving back; taking care of yourself and others, healthy or unhealthy boundaries, self-care; empathizing, understanding how others feel; shame, guilt, remorse; hiding, denying, avoiding, resisting; deflecting, projecting; revealing, disclosing, exposing; releasing, integrating; invisible, unseen; dark, destructive; despair, desolation.

I am whole, well and complete.

PISCES

FORM: Go forth into matter.
SOUL: I leave the Father's Home and turning back, I save.

Magenta

DIVINE LOVE, ATTENTION TO DETAIL, THE LITTLE THINGS, COMPASSION

Love from above, infinite love, grace, mercy; love merged with service, selflessness; treating others with kindness, empathy and compassion; awareness and appreciation of the little things, applying love and care to minor details; being mindful and present; conscious, aware, awake, alert; searching for love outside the human experience, the angelic realm, other realms; soul star.

I am the mindful, detached observer.

AFFIRMATION: I am a loving strand in the stream of divine love.

From out of the crucible of human experience the pure white peaks of the Mountain stand revealed. From here, the ringing of crystalline bells wafts over the valleys, arising in symphonic colour and sound.
The reason for turning to metaphor ... is to prepare you to enter a realm where you will experience subtly distinct frequencies of colour, sound, and currents of energy, which will infuse the soul with the joy of revelation. To learn to hear the shimmering essences of Life is to tread the path of higher evolution into the coming age.
Messages from Kanchenjunga 2015, 26

Bibliography

Bailey, Alice. 1942. *A Treatise on the Seven Rays Volume 2: Esoteric Psychology.* New York: Lucis Trust.

Bailey, Alice. 1950. *Letters on Occult Meditation.* New York: Lucis Trust.

Bailey, Alice. 1951. *A Treatise on the Seven Rays Volume 3: Esoteric Astrology.* New York: Lucis Trust.

Bailey, Alice. 1951. *The Unfinished Autobiography.* New York: Lucis Trust.

Bailey, Alice. 1960. *A Treatise on the Seven Rays Volume 5: The Rays and the Initiations.* New York: Lucis Trust.

Bailey, Alice. 1979. *A Treatise on Cosmic Fire.* New York: Lucis Trust.

Bayliss, Stephen. 2016. "Introduction to Astrology" (Powerpoint). Sydney: Author.

Besant, Annie. 1892. *The Seven Principles of Man* (2nd ed). London: Theosophical Publishing Society. Retrieved from http://ia802606.us.archive.org/34/items/sevenprinciples01besagoog/sevenprinciples01besagoog.pdf.

Blavatsky, Helena. 1888. *The Secret Doctrine Volume 1*. London: The Theosophical Publishing Co, Ltd. Retrieved from http://www.theosociety.org/pasadena/sd-pdf/SecretDoctrineVol1_eBook.pdf.

Blavatsky, Helena. Late 1800s. *The Secret Doctrine Volume 3*. Retrieved from http://cdn.website-editor.net/e4d6563c50794969b714ab70457d9761/files/uploaded/SecretDoctrine,The_HPBlavatsky.pdf.

Booth, Mike. 2000. *Aura-Soma Handbook*. England: Author.

Booth, Mike & McKnight, Carol. 2006. *The Aura-Soma Sourcebook: Color Therapy for the Soul*. Rochester: Healing Arts Press.

"Call from The Mountain." 2015. Retrieved from http://www.callfromthemountain.net/wp-content/uploads/2015/05/Call_from_the_Mountain.pdf.

Elliot, Andrew. 2015. "Color and psychological functioning: a review of theoretical and empirical work." Front. Psychol. Retrieved from http://doi.org/10.3389/fpsyg.2015.00368.

Evans, Jane. 1979. *Twelve Doors to the Soul*. Wheaton: The Theosophical Publishing House (Quest Books).

H.P.B. 1889. *The Voice of the Silence*. London: The Theosophical Publishing Co, Ltd. Retrieved from http://blavatskyarchives.com/theosophypdfs/blavatsky__the_voice_of_the_silence_1889.pdf.

"Instructions on Group Discipleship." 2015. Retrieved from http://www.callfromthemountain.net/wp-content/uploads/2015/05/Instructions-on-Group-Discipleship.pdf.

Lucis. n.d. "Mantrums." Retrieved from http://www.lucistrust.org/mantrams.

Lucis. n.d. "The Books of Alice Bailey: Discipleship in the New Age, Vol. II. Section Four - Personal Instructions To Disciples Part 13." Retrieved from http://www.lucistrust.org/online_books/discipleship_in_the_new_age_vol_ii_obooks/section_four_personal_instructions_disciples_part13.

Lucis. n.d. "The Great Invocation: Adapted Great Invocation." Retrieved from http://www.lucistrust.org/the_great_invocation/adapted_great_invocation.

Meader, William. 2004. *Shine Forth: The Soul's Magical Destiny*. Mariposa: Source Publications.

Meader, William. 2013. "Esoteric Astrology: The Revealer of the Soul's Intention." Retrieved from http://meader.org/articles/esoteric-astrology-the-revealer-of-the-souls-intention/.

Meader, William. 2013. "The World of Meaning: The Circumstantial Revelations of the Soul." Retrieved from http://meader.org/articles/the-world-of-meaning-the-circumstantial-revelations-of-the-soul/.

"Messages from Kanchenjunga." 2015. Retrieved from http://www.callfromthemountain.net/wp-content/uploads/2015/05/Messages-from-Kanchenjunga.pdf.

Montessori, Maria. 1967. *The Absorbent Mind*. New York: Holt Rinehart & Winston.

The Tibetan. 1943. *My Work*. London: Lucis Trust.

Wightman, I. 2006. "The texts of Alice A Bailey: An inquiry into the role of esotericism into transforming consciousness." PhD diss., University of Western Sydney.

World Goodwill. n.d. *The Great Invocation: The Use and Significance of The Great Invocation*. London: Author.

Peace to all Beings

www.ingramcontent.com/pod-product-compliance
Lightning Source LLC
Chambersburg PA
CBHW041500010526
44107CB00044B/1514